LET'S LEARN ABOUT...
THE LAND

PROJECT BOOK

STEAM

K2

Pearson

Pearson Education Limited
KAO Two, KAO Park, Harlow, Essex, CM17 9NA, England
and Associated Companies around the world

First published 2020

ISBN: 978-1-292-33451-6

Set in Mundo Sans
Printed in China SWTC/01

Acknowledgements
The publishers and author(s) would like to thank the following people and institutions for their feedback and comments during the development of the material: Marcos Mendonça, Leandra Dias, Gisele Aga, Viviane Kirmeliene, Rhiannon Ball, Mônica Bicalho and GB Editorial. The publishers would also like to thank all the teachers who contributed to the development of *Let's learn about...*: Adriano de Paula Souza, Aline Ramos Teixeira Santo, Aline Vitor Rodrigues Pina Pereira, Ana Paula Gomez Montero, Anna Flávia Feitosa Passos, Camila Jarola, Celiane Junker Silva, Edegar França Junior, Fabiana Reis Yoshio, Fernanda de Souza Thomaz, Luana da Silva, Michael Iacovino Luidvinavicius, Munique Dias de Melo, Priscila Rossatti Duval Ferreira Neves, Sandra Ferito, and schools that took part in Construindo Juntos.

Author Acknowledgements
Luciana Pinheiro and Simara H. Dal'Alba

Image Credit(s):
Pearson Education Ltd: 5, 7, 11, 13, 13, 17, 17, 19, 21, 23, 25, 45, 49, 53, 57, 59, 63, 67, 71, 73, 75, 83, 85, 87, MRS Editorial 44, 44, 44, 44, Sheila Cabeza de Vaca 65;
Shutterstock.com: Akhmad Dody Firmansyah 15, Anatolii Riepin 51, Ann679 35, Art Alex 31, AtlasStudio 15, BaLL LunLa 15, Fetullah Mercan 27, Fotinia 33, Gts 51, Julien Tromeur 39, Karpov Ilia 55, Kyselova Inna 51, Lauritta 39, Mama Belle and the kids 15, MyImages - Micha 15, Mything 39, Nelea33 51, New Africa 51, Sabelskaya 43, Sunnydream 55, Vietnam Stock Images 15, Yevgen Kravchenko 43.

Illustration Acknowledgements
Illustrated by Filipe Laurentino and MRS Editorial

Cover illustration © Filipe Laurentino

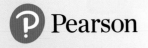

CONTENTS

U1 WHAT DO YOU LIKE ABOUT YOURSELF?   5

U2 WHY DO WE GO TO SCHOOL?   13

U3 HOW CAN YOU HELP YOUR FAMILY AT HOME?   21

U4 WHY DO WE FEEL HOT OR COLD?   29

U5 WHAT OTHER LIVING THINGS ARE AROUND US?   37

U6 WHY IS FOOD IMPORTANT?   45

U7 HOW CAN FARM ANIMALS HELP US?   53

U8 WHO LIVES AND WORKS IN MY TOWN?   61

STICKERS   81

DRAW ARROWS TO ORDER THE STORY. SAY.

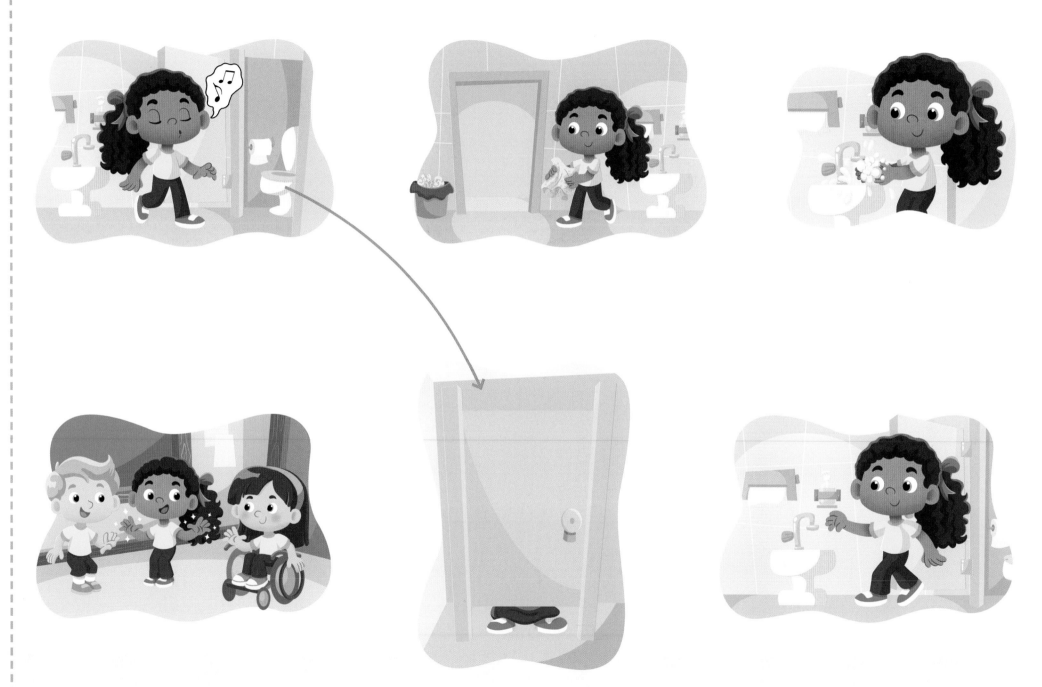

COLOR AND CUT OUT THE HAND. GLUE A TISSUE.

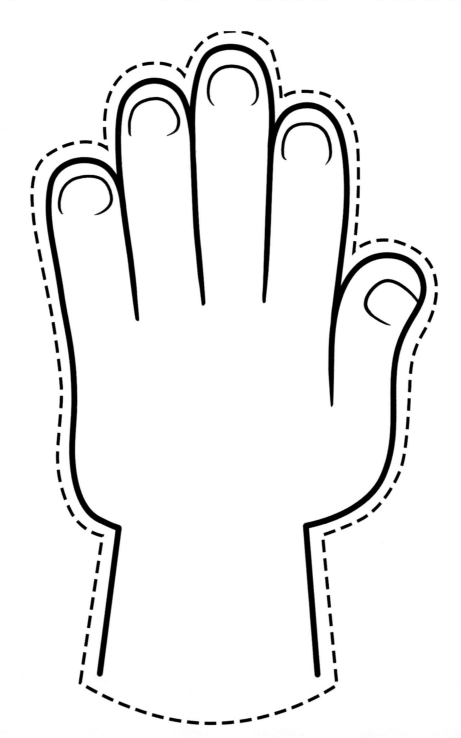

WHAT IF YOUR FACE WAS DIFFERENT? DRAW AND COLOR. SAY.

LOOK AND STICK. WHAT IS THE BOY DOING?

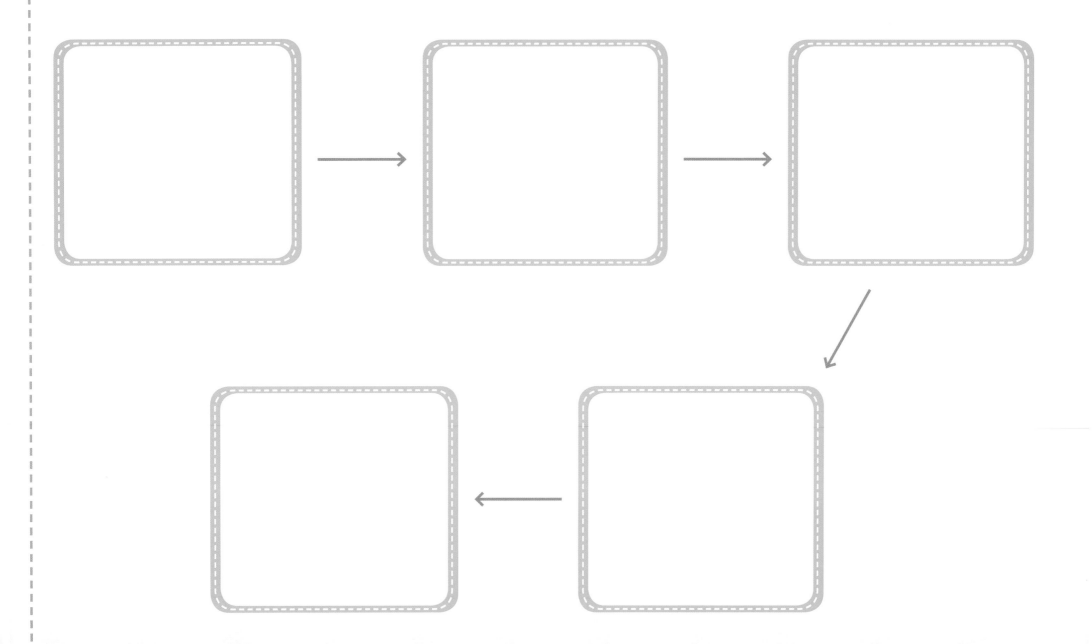

PLAY THE RECYCLING GAME. COLOR THE ITEMS GREEN OR YELLOW.

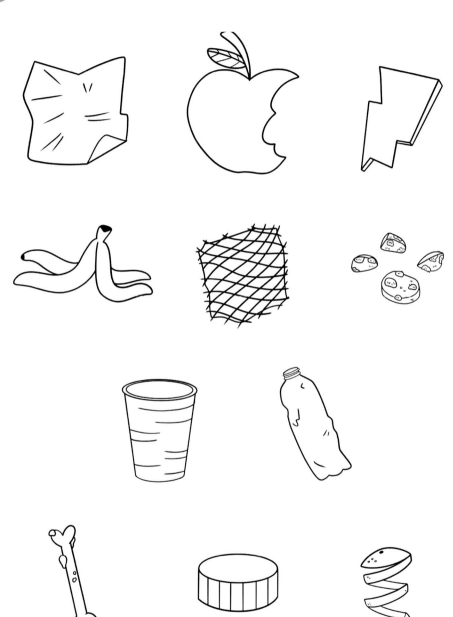

WHICH ITEMS ARE MADE FROM RECYCLABLE MATERIALS? CIRCLE.

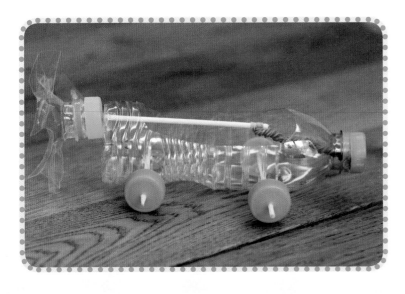

COUNT AND COLOR THE CIRCLES ON EACH MUSICAL INSTRUMENT. 3 ✏️

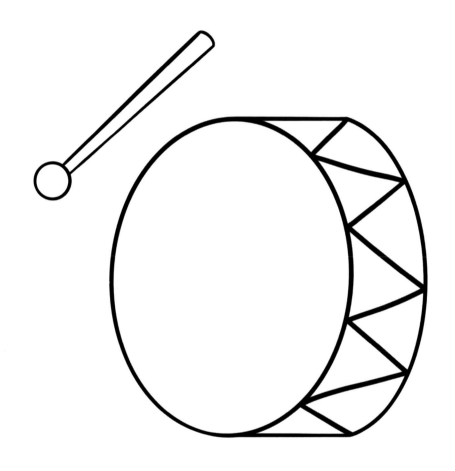

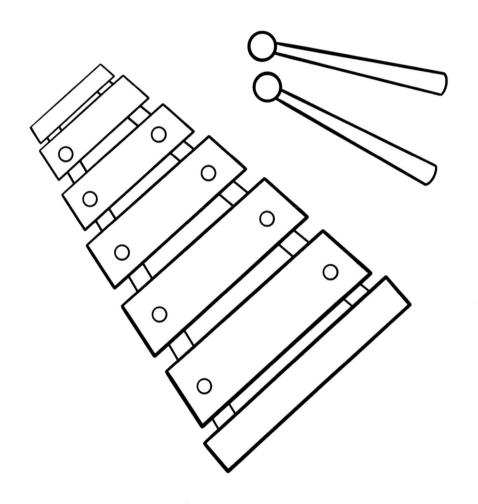

IDENTIFY THE BUGS IN THIS SCHOOL ROUTINE. CROSS THEM OUT. 👁 X

START

FINISH

DRAW ARROWS TO ORDER THE STORY.

LOOK AT THE OUTLINES. STICK AND SAY.

HELP MOMMY DUCK FIND HER LITTLE DUCKS. COUNT AND SAY.

CHOOSE A FAMILY MEMBER. WRITE THE LETTER AND THE BINARY CODE.

RECORD HERE THE RESULTS OF YOUR RAINBOW REFLECTION EXPERIMENT.

WHICH THERMOMETER SHOWS COLD WEATHER? CIRCLE.

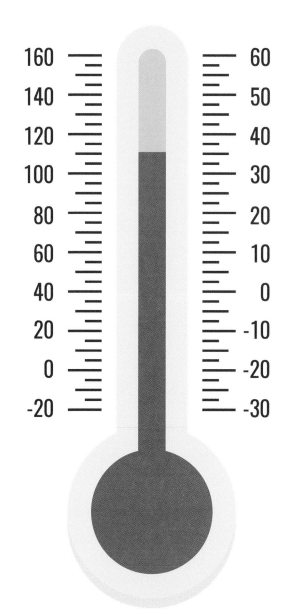

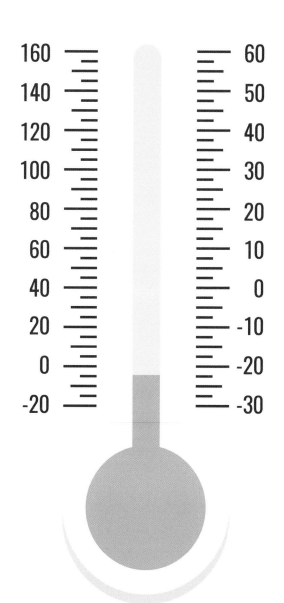

CUT OUT THE PICTURES. PLAY A SORTING-OUT GAME.

MAKE A NATURE ARTWORK.

STICK THE PICTURES TO SHOW THE POLLINATION PROCESS.

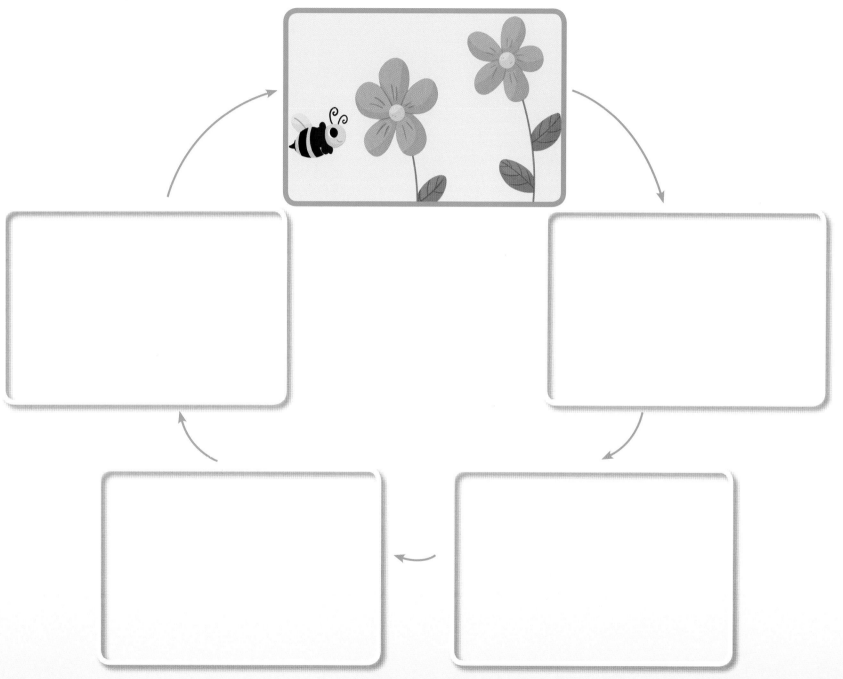

LOOK AND CROSS OUT THE BUGS IN THE HONEYCOMB.  X

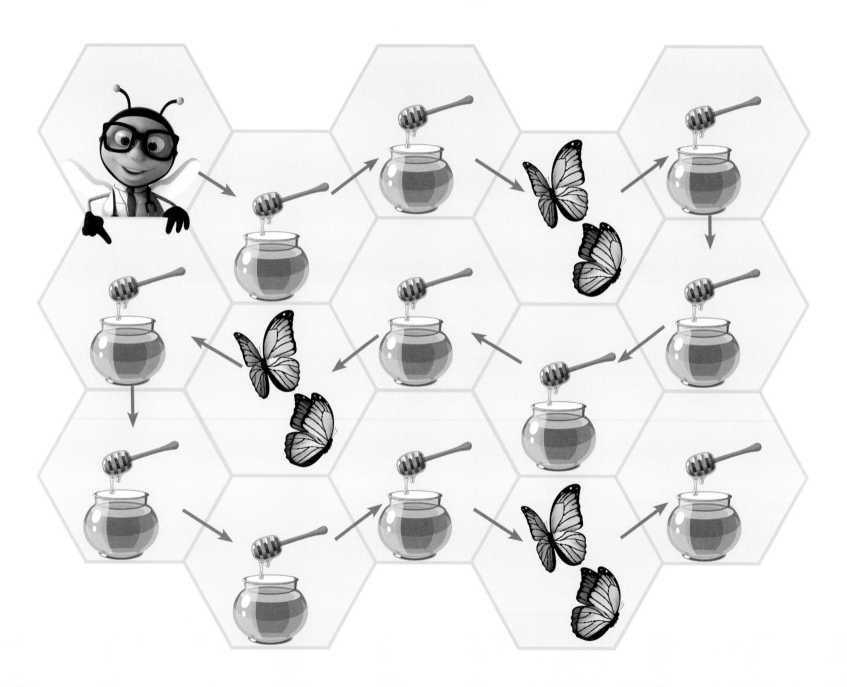

MATCH THE ANIMALS WITH THEIR FOOTPRINTS.

HELP THE SPIDER GET TO THE WEB.

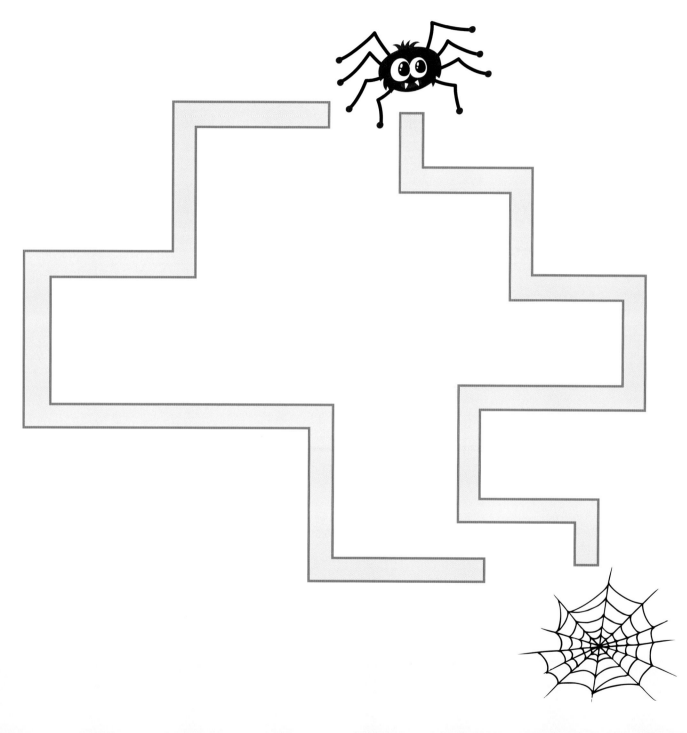

WHAT CAN CLEAN YOUR HANDS? CIRCLE THEM BLUE.

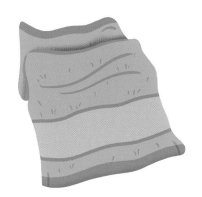

RECORD THE PROGRESS OF YOUR EXPERIMENT.

BEFORE	AFTER AN HOUR	THE NEXT DAY

WHICH CONTAINER CAN'T YOU USE TO PUT RAVIOLI IN THE FREEZER? CROSS IT OUT.

WHICH FOOD DO YOU USUALLY EAT COLD? CIRCLE THEM BLUE.

CONNECT THE SHAPES TO MAKE WINGS ON THE ROBOT CHICK. WHAT'S THE CODE?

LOOK AND COUNT. HOW MANY CHICKS ARE MISSING? DRAW.   3

WHAT ANIMALS ARE MISSING? FOLLOW THE SEQUENCE OF THE SONG AND DRAW.

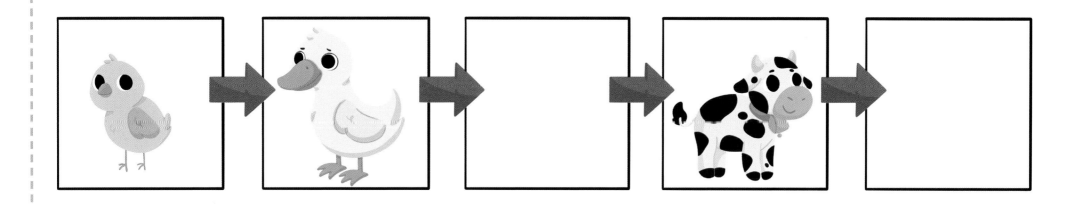

MAKE COLORFUL SHEEP WOOL.

COMPARE YOUR CRAFT TOWN TO YOUR SCHOOL NEIGHBORHOOD. DRAW ONE DIFFERENCE.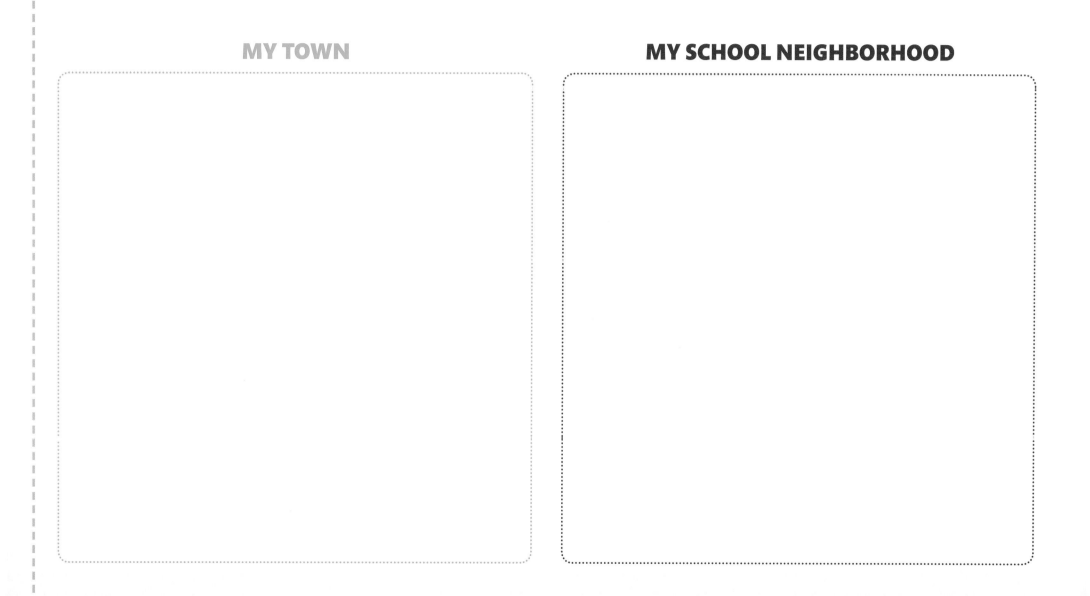

MY TOWN

MY SCHOOL NEIGHBORHOOD

USE ARROWS TO CHOOSE THE RAILWAY FOR THE TRAIN.

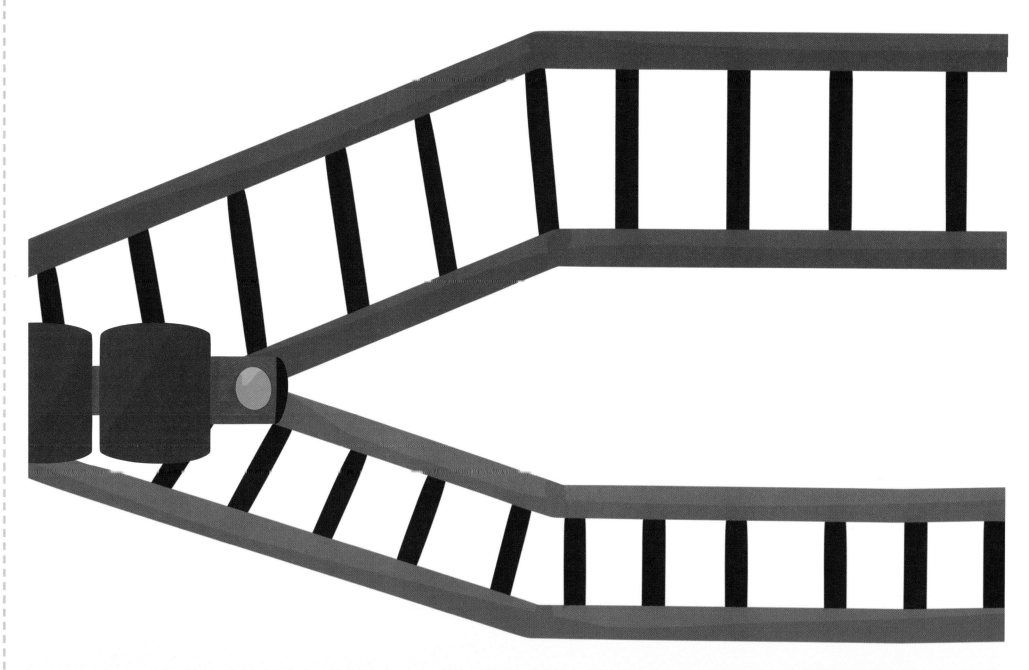

LOOK AND SAY. WHAT'S MISSING? GLUE.

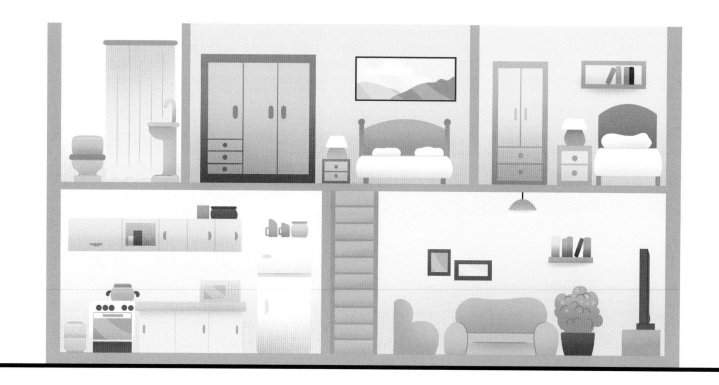

MAKE A BEAUTIFUL GARDEN FOR THE HOUSE.

WHICH LADDER IS JUST RIGHT TO SAVE THE CAT? LOOK AND CIRCLE.

DRAWING

DRAW.

DRAW.

DRAW.

DRAW.

DRAW.

STICKERS

STICKERS
UNIT 1

STICKERS
UNIT 3

STICKERS

UNIT 5

UNIT 8